UNITED STATES
TRIVIA
FOR KIDS

BY ELIZABETH JAMES

Published in the United States by Big Heart Books.

BIG HEART
books

TABLE OF CONTENTS

EXCLUSIVE FREEBIE!

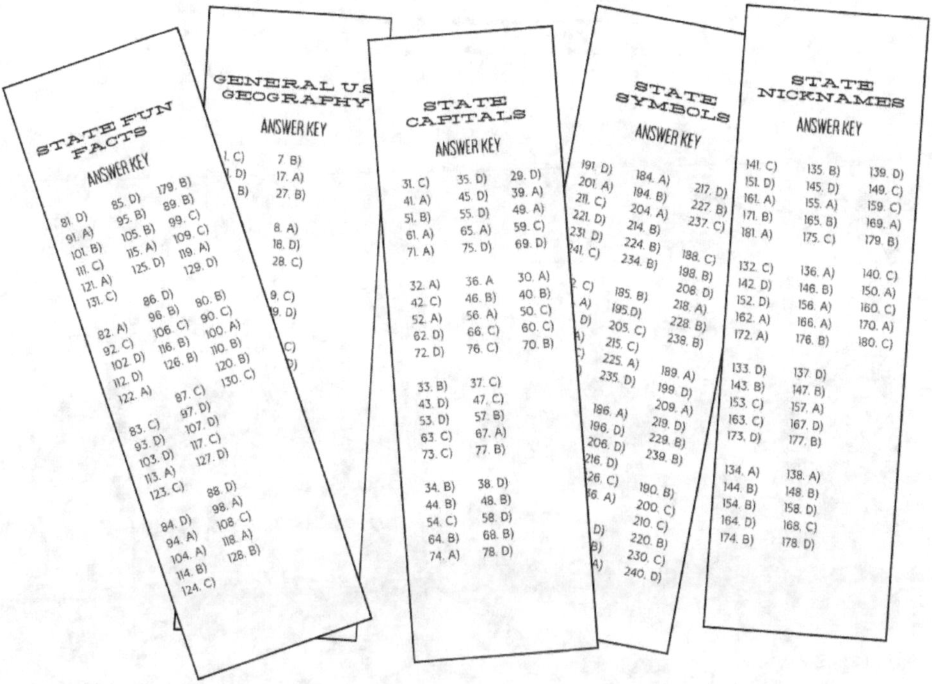

STATE FUN FACTS
ANSWER KEY

GENERAL U.S. GEOGRAPHY
ANSWER KEY

STATE CAPITALS
ANSWER KEY

STATE SYMBOLS
ANSWER KEY

STATE NICKNAMES
ANSWER KEY

GET ALL THE ANSWERS AT YOUR FINGERTIPS!

DOWNLOAD FREE PRINTABLE ANSWER KEY BOOKMARKS

WHEN YOU SIGN UP FOR EMAILS!

Visit elizabethjameswrites.com/USAfreebie

HAVE EVEN MORE TRIVIA FUN!

FUN FACTS ABOUT SCIENCE: 240+ **TRIVIA QUESTIONS** FOR KIDS AGES 8-12

TEST YOUR KNOWLEDGE WITH 240+ MULTIPLE-CHOICE, FUN-FILLED QUESTIONS ABOUT PLANTS, ANIMALS, THE HUMAN BODY, EARTH & OUTER SPACE!

ELIZABETH JAMES

TRIVIA TO-GO FAMILY CHALLENGE 240+ **TRIVIA QUESTIONS** HOLIDAY EDITION

CELEBRATE ALL YOUR FAVORITE HOLIDAYS WITH FESTIVE, MULTIPLE-CHOICE TRIVIA Q&A GAMES FOR ON-THE-GO FUN FOR THE WHOLE FAMILY!

ELIZABETH JAMES

MAKE LEARNING ABOUT SCIENCE FEEL LIKE A GAME!

LEARN ALL ABOUT YOUR FAVORITE HOLIDAYS!

INTRODUCTION

The United States of America is one of the largest countries in the world, covering more than 3 million square miles! That's a lot of area—which is why we wrote this book: to make learning about the 50 states fun!

We've compiled the most interesting facts about every state (and even the five major U.S. territories) and turned them into interactive trivia questions you can use to unlock your knowledge about the United States. Multiple-choice answers make it easy for everyone to play along.

The questions are organized into five different topics: general US geography for kids; USA states and capitals; fun facts about all 50 states for kids; state nicknames as well as various state symbols. (Check out the appendix for lists of state capitals, nicknames and official animals, flowers, birds, and more!)

Plus, we've also included 5 different game challenges to make the learning even more fun as you make your way through this United States kids book.

Now, let your United States trivia adventure begin!

GENERAL U.S. GEOGRAPHY

1. How many states are there in the United States of America?
A) 48
B) 49
C) 50
D) 51

2. Which of the following is a state?
A) Portland
B) Maryland
C) Cleveland
D) Oakland

3. Which of the following is *not* a state?
A) New Orleans
B) New Mexico
C) New Hampshire
D) New Jersey

ANSWERS ON PAGE 106

4. Which state was the first state to join the United States on Dec. 7, 1787?

A) Massachusetts

B) Delaware

C) Virginia

D) New York

5. Which state was the last state to join the United States on Aug. 21, 1959?

A) Alaska

B) Texas

C) California

D) Hawaii

6. Which state has the largest population (or number of residents)?

A) California

B) Texas

C) Florida

D) New York

7. Sometimes when we talk about the U.S. states, we say that some states are part of the "contiguous U.S." and some are part of the "non-contiguous U.S." What does contiguous mean?

A) The states that are all along the coast

B) The states that are all next to each other

C) The states that have the most people

D) The states that don't freeze in winter

8. How many contiguous states are there?

A) 48
B) 49
C) 50
D) 51

9. Which of the following states are non-contiguous states?

A) Florida and Texas
B) New York and California
C) Alaska and Hawaii
D) Washington and Maine

10. Which mountain peak is the tallest in the United States?

A) Grand Teton (Wyoming)
B) Mount Rainier (Washington)
C) Denali (Alaska)
D) Mount Whitney (California)

11. Which river is the longest in the United States?

A) Mississippi River
B) Ohio River
C) Colorado River
D) Missouri River

12. Which ocean is on the West Coast of the United States?

A) Atlantic Ocean
B) Pacific Ocean
C) Indian Ocean
D) Arctic Ocean

ANSWERS ON PAGE 106

13. What is the name of the major mountain range that runs along the eastern United States?
A) Rocky Mountains
B) Sierra Nevada
C) Appalachian Mountains
D) Cascade Range

14. Why is a state capital important?
A) It's where the state government is located
B) It's were the most people in the state are located
C) It's where the oldest city in the state is located
D) It's where the most jobs in the state are located

15. Just like each state has its own capital city, the United States also has a capital city. Which city is the capital city of the U.S.?
A) Los Angeles
B) New York
C) Washington D.C.
D) Chicago

16. Washington DC is not part of any state, but instead is a federal _____?
A) District
B) County
C) Municipality
D) Province

17. During his presidency, George Washington selected an area along the Potomac River to become Washington DC. What is one of the major reasons he selected this location?

A) It was considered a neutral area between northern and southern states.
B) It provided a good lookout spot over the Atlantic Ocean.
C) It was one of the oldest cities in the new nation.
D) It was well protected in case of attack.

18. Many residents of Washington DC want the city to be its own state. What is one of their main reasons for this?
A) They want to design their own state flag.
B) They want to be able to elect their own mayor.
C) They want to be able to have their own license plates.
D) They pay taxes without getting to have full representation in Congress.

19. In addition to the 50 states in the U.S., there are other places that the U.S. helps take care of, but they are not states. These places are called territories. What is the main difference between a state and a territory?
A) Territories are larger than states.
B) States are only on the mainland.
C) Territories don't have any people living in them.
D) States have full representation in the U.S. Congress.

20. Three of the following statements are true about U.S. territories. Which one is *not* true about U.S. territories?
A) They all pay some taxes to the U.S. government.
B) They all are islands or groups of islands.

ANSWERS ON PAGE 106

C) They all can travel freely within the United States.

D) They all can vote for the U.S. President.

21. Which of the following is a state, *not* a U.S. territory?

A) U.S. Virgin Islands

B) Rhode Island

C) Norther Mariana Islands

D) Puerto Rico

22. The U.S. has 16 territories, but only five have people living there all the time. These five are called major territories, and the other 11 are called Minor Outlying Islands. Three of the following are major territories; which one is a U.S. minor territory?

A) Guam

B) Baker Island

C) U.S. Virgin Islands

D) Northern Mariana Islands

23. Of the five major U.S. territories, two have been territories the longest—since 1898, when they became U.S. territories after the Spanish-American War. One of those territories is Guam; what is the other one?

A) Puerto Rico

B) U.S. Virgin Islands

C) Northern Mariana Islands

D) American Samoa

24. The nation's newest territory has only been an official U.S. territory since 1975, even though the U.S.

has been in control of these islands since World War II. Which territory is it?

A) Puerto Rico
B) U.S. Virgin Islands
C) Northern Mariana Islands
D) American Samoa

25. Which U.S. territory did the U.S. purchase in 1917 from the country of Denmark—for $25 million in gold?!

A) Puerto Rico
B) U.S. Virgin Islands
C) Northern Mariana Islands
D) American Samoa

26. Four of the major U.S. territories are in the Northern Hemisphere, north of the equator. Which is the only U.S. territory located in the Southern Hemisphere?

A) Puerto Rico
B) U.S. Virgin Islands
C) Northern Mariana Islands
D) American Samoa

27. People born in a U.S. territory are considered U.S. citizens except on this territory, where they are born as U.S. nationals but must take a test to become a U.S. citizen. Which territory is it?

A) Guam
B) American Samoa
C) U.S. Virgin Islands
D) Puerto Rico

ANSWERS ON PAGE 106

28. A lot of states used to be territories before they became states. But some states, like the 13 original colonies, were never territories—they just became states on their own. Three of the following states were not territories; they broke off from already-existing states. Which of the following states *did* enter the U.S. as a territory?

A) Kentucky
B) Maine
C) New Mexico
D) West Virginia

THE 20 POINT CHALLENGE

Test your knowledge by answering trivia questions correctly and being the first to reach 20 points!

Number of Players: 1 or more

Instructions:
- Pass out a piece of paper and a writing utensil to each player.
- Determine which category you will read questions from.
- Read 10 questions out loud at a time, with all players recording their own answers at this time. (One person may read all of the questions, or players may take turns reading them out loud. If desired, use a timer for recording responses.)
- Once all 10 questions have been read, look up the answers in the back of the book. Each participant may score their own sheets, or they may exchange them for scoring purposes.
- Each correct answer equals one point.
- Play additional rounds and score those questions until one player reaches 20 points—making them the winner!

STATE CAPITALS

29. All the following cities are found in Alabama. Which one is Alabama's state capital?
A) Birmingham
B) Mobile
C) Huntsville
D) Montgomery

30. All the following cities are found in Alaska. Which one is Alaska's state capital?
A) Juneau
B) Anchorage
C) Fairbanks
D) Valdez

31. All the following cities are found in Arizona. Which one is Arizona's state capital?
A) Tucson
B) Mesa
C) Phoenix
D) Scottsdale

32. All the following cities are found in Arkansas. Which one is Arkansas's state capital?
A) Little Rock
B) Fayetteville
C) Fort Smith
D) Jonesboro

33. All the following cities are found in California. Which one is California's state capital?
A) Los Angeles
B) Sacramento
C) San Diego
D) San Francisco

34. All the following cities are found in Colorado. Which one is Colorado's state capital?
A) Colorado Springs
B) Denver
C) Aurora
D) Fort Collins

35. All the following cities are found in Connecticut. Which one is Connecticut's state capital?
A) New Haven
B) Bridgeport
C) Stamford
D) Hartford

36. All the following cities are found in Delaware. Which one is Delaware's state capital?
A) Dover
B) Wilmington

ANSWERS ON PAGE 106

C) Newark

D) Middletown

37. All the following cities are found in Florida. Which one is Florida's state capital?

A) Miami

B) Orlando

C) Tallahassee

D) Jacksonville

38. All the following cities are found in Georgia. Which one is Georgia's state capital?

A) Augusta

B) Savannah

C) Macon

D) Atlanta

39. All the following cities are found in Hawaii. Which one is Hawaii's state capital?

A) Honolulu

B) Hilo

C) Kailua

D) Pearl City

40. All the following cities are found in Idaho. Which one is Idaho's state capital?

A) Idaho Falls

B) Boise

C) Nampa

D) Meridian

41. All the following cities are found in Illinois. Which one is Illinois's state capital?

A) Springfield
B) Chicago
C) Aurora
D) Naperville

42. All the following cities are found in Indiana. Which one is Indiana's state capital?
A) Fort Wayne
B) Evansville
C) Indianapolis
D) South Bend

43. All the following cities are found in Iowa. Which one is Iowa's state capital?
A) Cedar Rapids
B) Davenport
C) Iowa City
D) Des Moines

44. All the following cities are found in Kansas. Which one is Kansas's state capital?
A) Wichita
B) Topeka
C) Overland Park
D) Kansas City

45. All the following cities are found in Kentucky. Which one is Kentucky's state capital?
A) Louisville
B) Lexington
C) Bowling Green
D) Frankfort

ANSWERS ON PAGE 106

46. All the following cities are found in Louisiana. Which one is Louisiana's state capital?
A) New Orleans
B) Baton Rouge
C) Shreveport
D) Lafayette

47. All the following cities are found in Maine. Which one is Maine's state capital?
A) Portland
B) Bangor
C) Augusta
D) Lewiston

48. All the following cities are found in Maryland. Which one is Maryland's state capital?
A) Baltimore
B) Annapolis
C) Columbia
D) Waldorf

49. All the following cities are found in Massachusetts. Which one is Massachusetts's state capital?
A) Boston
B) Worcester
C) Springfield
D) Cambridge

50. All the following cities are found in Michigan. Which one is Michigan's state capital?
A) Detroit
B) Grand Rapids

C) Lansing
D) Ann Arbor

51. All the following cities are found in Minnesota. Which one is Minnesota's state capital?
A) Minneapolis
B) Saint Paul
C) Rochester
D) Duluth

52. All the following cities are found in Mississippi. Which one is Mississippi's state capital?
A) Jackson
B) Gulfport
C) Hattiesburg
D) Biloxi

53. All the following cities are found in Missouri. Which one is Missouri's state capital?
A) Independence
B) Saint Louis
C) Springfield
D) Jefferson City

54. All the following cities are found in Montana. Which one is Montana's state capital?
A) Billings
B) Bozeman
C) Helena
D) Great Falls

ANSWERS ON PAGE 106

55. All the following cities are found in Nebraska. Which one is Nebraska's state capital?
A) Grand Island
B) Omaha
C) Bellevue
D) Lincoln

56. All the following cities are found in Nevada. Which one is Nevada's state capital?
A) Carson City
B) Las Vegas
C) Reno
D) Henderson

57. All the following cities are found in New Hampshire. Which one is New Hampshire's state capital?
A) Manchester
B) Concord
C) Nashua
D) Rochester

58. All the following cities are found in New Jersey. Which one is New Jersey's state capital?
A) Paterson
B) Newark
C) Jersey City
D) Trenton

59. All the following cities are found in New Mexico. Which one is New Mexico's state capital?

A) Albuquerque
B) Rio Rancho
C) Santa Fe
D) Roswell

60. All the following cities are found in New York. Which one is New York's state capital?
A) New York City
B) Buffalo
C) Albany
D) Syracuse

61. All the following cities are found in North Carolina. Which one is North Carolina's state capital?
A) Raleigh
B) Charlotte
C) Greensboro
D) Durham

62. All the following cities are found in North Dakota. Which one is North Dakota's state capital?
A) Minot
B) Fargo
C) Grand Forks
D) Bismarck

63. All the following cities are found in Ohio. Which one is Ohio's state capital?
A) Cleveland
B) Cincinnati
C) Columbus
D) Toledo

ANSWERS ON PAGE 106

64. All the following cities are found in Oklahoma. Which one is Oklahoma's state capital?
A) Tulsa
B) Oklahoma City
C) Norman
D) Broken Arrow

65. All the following cities are found in Oregon. Which one is Oregon's state capital?
A) Salem
B) Portland
C) Eugene
D) Gresham

66. All the following cities are found in Pennsylvania. Which one is Pennsylvania's state capital?
A) Philadelphia
B) Pittsburgh
C) Harrisburg
D) Allentown

67. All the following cities are found in Rhode Island. Which one is Rhode Island's state capital?
A) Providence
B) Warwick
C) Cranston
D) Pawtucket

68. All the following cities are found in South Carolina. Which one is South Carolina's state capital?
A) Charleston
B) Columbia

C) Greenville
D) Spartanburg

69. All the following cities are found in South Dakota. Which one is South Dakota's state capital?
A) Sioux Falls
B) Rapid City
C) Aberdeen
D) Pierre

70. All the following cities are found in Tennessee. Which one is Tennessee's state capital?
A) Memphis
B) Nashville
C) Knoxville
D) Chattanooga

71. All the following cities are found in Texas. Which one is Texas's state capital?
A) Austin
B) Houston
C) Dallas
D) San Antonio

72. All the following cities are found in Utah. Which one is Utah's state capital?
A) Moab
B) Provo
C) Park City
D) Salt Lake City

ANSWERS ON PAGE 106

73. All the following cities are found in Vermont. Which one is Vermont's state capital?
A) Burlington
B) Rutland
C) Montpelier
D) Bennington

74. All the following cities are found in Virginia. Which one is Virginia's state capital?
A) Richmond
B) Arlington
C) Norfolk
D) Chesapeake

75. All the following cities are found in Washington. Which one is Washington's state capital?
A) Seattle
B) Spokane
C) Tacoma
D) Olympia

76. All the following cities are found in West Virginia. Which one is West Virginia's state capital?
A) Huntington
B) Morgantown
C) Charleston
D) Parkersburg

77. All the following cities are found in Wisconsin. Which one is Wisconsin's state capital?

A) Milwaukee
B) Madison
C) Green Bay
D) Racine

78. All the following cities are found in Wyoming. Which one is Wyoming's state capital?
A) Gillette
B) Casper
C) Laramie
D) Cheyenne

ANSWERS ON PAGE 106

GAME #2

SHOWDOWN CHALLENGE

How much does your opponent know? Find out with this game that involves selecting questions to put other teams to the test!

Number of Players: 2 or more (individually or as teams)

Instructions:
- Determine which category you will read questions from and for how many rounds you will play.
- The first player (or team) to go can be determined by flipping a coin, playing "Rock, Paper, Scissors" or another method.
- Players will take turns selecting a question for their opponent(s), and then read that question and multiple-choice options aloud. The guessing player(s) will select an answer within a set amount of time.
- Correct responses are worth one point. Tally players' scores.
- The next player (or team) will select a question for their opponent(s), and play will continue like this until all players have taken an equal number of turns reading questions.
- The team or player with the highest score at the end of the last round wins.

FUN STATE FACTS

79. This state is bordered by the Missouri River to the west and the Mississippi River to the east. It has some of the best soil in the world and grows the most corn in the country. Not surprisingly, farmland covers 92 percent of the state! Which state is it?
A) Illinois
B) Iowa
C) Kansas
D) Arkansas

80. This state originally was part of the Virginia colony and is named after Virginian governor, Lord De La Warr. It is the second-smallest state and borders the Atlantic Ocean. It also has a river and bay that share its name, as well as find the Great Cypress Swamp, the northernmost cypress swamp in the U.S. with trees that are hundreds of years old. Which state is it?

ANSWERS ON PAGE 107

A) Maine
B) Delaware
C) Vermont
D) New Hampshire

81. This state's name comes from the Spanish word for "mountains," and it has more than 3,000 of them! It's also where you'll find glaciers in Glacier National Park, ancient pictograph drawings at Pictograph Cave State Park, and the Little Bighorn Battlefield where Sitting Bull and Lt. Colonel Custer fought. Which state is it?
A) Alaska
B) Wisconsin
C) South Dakota
D) Montana

82. This mitten-shaped state borders four of the five Great Lakes and is famous for its role in the car industry. It's where car companies like Ford, Buick, Dodge and Chrysler started and the city of Detroit became known as "the car capital of the world." Which state is it?
A) Michigan
B) New York
C) South Carolina
D) Maine

83. This state is famous for the Roswell crash site, where some people think a UFO landed (but others say it was just a weather balloon). It's also where the first atomic bomb was created and tested during

World War II, as well as Carlsbad Caverns (home to thousands of bats), ancient Pueblo ruins (where they even found mummies), and the biggest hot-air balloon event in the world. Which state is it?

A) Texas
B) Oklahoma
C) New Mexico
D) Nevada

84. This state is known as "the breadbasket of America" because it grows a lot of the country's wheat and sorghum. It's also famous for a movie that features this state with Judy Garland that came out in 1939. Which state is it?

A) Indiana
B) Oregon
C) Virginia
D) Kansas

85. This state used to be part of New York, but in 1777, it became its own republic for 14 years before joining the United States as the 14th state. Today, it makes about half of the country's maple syrup from its state tree, the sugar maple. Which state is it?

A) Massachusetts
B) Connecticut
C) Pennsylvania
D) Vermont

86. This state is where you'll find the "Theme Park Capital of the World," a city with more theme parks than anywhere else on Earth! It's also the only place in

ANSWERS ON PAGE 107

the world where alligators and crocodiles live together in Everglades National Park, the biggest tropical wilderness in the U.S. Which state is it?

A) California

B) Alabama

C) Hawaii

D) Florida

87. This state is known as "The Lighthouse State," even though Michigan has more lighthouses. It is where the Appalachian Trail through the Appalachian Mountains ends. It is also the state covered by the most forests—only 10 percent of its is *not* forested! Which state is it?

A) Alaska

B) Delaware

C) Maine

D) Ohio

88. This state is bordered by Lake Michigan to the north and the Mississippi River to the west. It's famous for deep-dish pizza, building the world's first skyscraper, and being called the "Land of Lincoln" because Abraham Lincoln lived here until he became president. Which state is it?

A) Minnesota

B) Indiana

C) Kentucky

D) Illinois

89. This state has the biggest city in the country. It's also where you'll find Niagara Falls, Catskill and

Adirondack Mountains, the Hudson River and the Statue of Liberty. Which state is it?
A) Wisconsin
B) New York
C) Maryland
D) California

90. This state is the only state bordered with rivers on three sides: the Ohio River to the north, the Mississippi River to the west, and the Big Sandy River and Tug Fork to the east. It's also where you'll find the longest-running sporting event in the country at Churchill Downs and the world's longest cave system, Mammoth Caves. Which state is it?
A) Ohio
B) Missouri
C) Kentucky
D) Mississippi

91. This state is the only one with all of the "Big Four" North American deserts: the Great Basin, Mojave, Sonoran, and Chihuahuan. These deserts include the largest hot desert (Chihuahuan) and the largest cold desert (Great Basin) in North America. It's also the only U.S. state to have one the seven natural wonders of the world: the Grand Canyon. Which state is it?
A) Arizona
B) New Mexico
C) Utah
D) Nevada

ANSWERS ON PAGE 107

92. In this state, you can visit the Biltmore House, the biggest privately-owned home in the country, and drive along part of the Blue Ridge Parkway through the Appalachian Highlands. But this state is most famous because the Wright brothers made their first flight here at Kitty Hawk in 1903. Which state is it?
A) Ohio
B) Nebraska
C) North Carolina
D) Washington

93. This is the second-biggest state in the country after Alaska. It has the most tornadoes and produces almost half of all the oil in the U.S.! One of its most famous landmarks is the Alamo, where settlers fought for independence from Mexico. Even though they lost, their bravery inspired others with the rallying cry, "Remember the Alamo!" Which state is it?
A) New Mexico
B) Arizona
C) Idaho
D) Texas

94. This state is home to the country's deepest lake, Crater Lake, which was formed when a huge volcano erupted 7,000 years ago and collapsed in on itself before filling with water. Located on the Pacific Coast, this state is also where you'll find Mount Hood and Multnomah Falls. Which state is it?
A) Oregon
B) Delaware
C) West Virginia
D) Georgia

95. This state is sometimes called "The Cotton State" because, at one time, it grew 23 percent of all the cotton in the country, even though Texas now grows more. It's also where civil rights leader Rosa Parks stood up for her rights by refusing to give up her bus seat in Montgomery. Which state is it?

A) Arkansas
B) Alabama
C) Nebraska
D) Louisiana

96. This state is where, at Jamestown in 1607, settlers established the first permanent European settlement in America. This state stretches all the way to the Atlantic Ocean and is home to the country's largest outdoor living museum, Colonial Williamsburg, where you can see what life was like in the 1700s. Which state is it?

A) Massachusetts
B) Virginia
C) Florida
D) New York

97. This state has the most National Parks in the country, even though it is also the state with the highest population. Some of the National Parks found here include Yosemite, Joshua Tree, and Death Valley. Which state is it?

A) Louisiana
B) North Dakota
C) Hawaii
D) California

ANSWERS ON PAGE 107

98. This state was the starting point for Lewis and Clark when they set out to explore the American West in 1804. Later on, many pioneers also began their journey west from here. That is why the world's tallest arch, the Gateway Arch is located here, on the western bank of the Mississippi River. Which state is it?

A) Missouri

B) West Virginia

C) Iowa

D) Kansas

99. This state was bought from Russia for two cents an acre! It has more coastline than all the other states combined and is one of the best places in the world to see the Northern Lights. It's also home to the tallest mountain in North America, Denali (formerly known as Mount McKinley), and the famous Iditarod Trail Sled Dog Race. Which state is it?

A) Minnesota

B) North Dakota

C) Alaska

D) Idaho

100. This state is famous for growing the most potatoes in the country. But it also has a giant waterfall on the Snake River that's sometimes called "the Niagara of the West." It's also home to Craters of the Moon National Monument & Preserve, a volcanic landscape that looks like the surface of the moon. Which state is it?

A) Idaho
B) Nebraska
C) Washington
D) Oregon

101. Even though this is one of the smallest states, it has a big role in our nation's history: It's where one of the most famous political protests happened (involving tea!) and where the Freedom Trail is located, which includes the Paul Revere House and America's oldest public park. Plus, this state is home to the oldest Major League Baseball stadium— Fenway Park! Which state is it?
A) Vermont
B) Massachusetts
C) New Hampshire
D) Rhode Island

102. This state is famous for its cheese, making 25 percent of all the cheese in the U.S.! It's bordered by both Lake Superior and Lake Michigan, and it's where the Ringling brothers started their first circus in 1884. The Fox River here is one of the few rivers in the country that flows north instead of south. It empties into Green Bay, where you'll also find the famous football stadium, Lambeau Field. Which state is it?
A) Illinois
B) Indiana
C) Michigan
D) Wisconsin

ANSWERS ON PAGE 107

103. This state is all about food! It's where you'll find the world's largest drive-in restaurant and the famous Vidalia onion, which can only be grown here. It's also home to the watermelon capital of the world and grows the most peanuts in the country. Former President Jimmy Carter grew up here as a peanut farmer and has a 13-foot-tall peanut sculpture outside his boyhood home! Which state is it?
A) Kentucky
B) Tennessee
C) South Carolina
D) Georgia

104. This state has both the most mountains and the driest climate in the U.S. It's where you'll find Lake Tahoe, the biggest alpine lake in the country, and Lake Mead, the largest man-made lake in the U.S. (which stretches into Arizona). It's also home to the city known as the "Entertainment Capital of the World," where there are so many neon lights that a NASA photo from outer space shows it's the brightest city on Earth. Which state is it?
A) Nevada
B) Oklahoma
C) California
D) New York

105. Located in the middle of the country, this state is known as the "Crossroads of America" because four major highways meet here. It's also famous for a 500-mile-long car race named after its capital city. This race is the oldest major car race in the world and is

called the "greatest spectacle in racing." Which state is it?

A) Iowa
B) Indiana
C) Kansas
D) Arkansas

106. This state, shaped like a cooking pot with a famous "panhandle," is at the end of the Trail of Tears, where many Native American tribes were relocated. Today, it's home to the largest number of Native American tribes in the country, with 39 tribes calling it home. You can also visit Black Mesa State Park to see ancient lava rocks and explore the Spiro Mounds, one of the most important Native American sites in the U.S. Which state is it?

A) Texas
B) South Dakota
C) Oklahoma
D) Idaho

107. Known as the "Diner Capital of the World" because it has more diners per person than any other state, this is also the most crowded state in the country. It's where Thomas Edison invented one of the first lightbulbs, and it's home to Atlantic City's famous boardwalk. This boardwalk was the first one ever built and is still the longest, oldest, and busiest boardwalk in the world. Which state is it?

A) Maryland
B) Connecticut
C) Georgia
D) New Jersey

ANSWERS ON PAGE 107

108. Some say this state looks like a frog, ready to jump over its southern neighbors, Kentucky and Virginia. It used to be part of Virginia until the Civil War when its people wanted to join the Union and fight against slavery. This state is also home to what might be the oldest river in North America, even though it's named the New River. Which state is it?
A) Maryland
B) Tennessee
C) West Virginia
D) New Hampshire

109. Named after the Ojibwe word "misi-ziibi," meaning "great river," this state is where the river it's named after finishes its journey. The river starts in Minnesota and flows through 10 states before reaching the Gulf of Mexico here. This state is also famous for where blues music and Memorial Day both started. Which state is it?
A) Michigan
B) Missouri
C) Mississippi
D) Montana

110. This state is made entirely of volcanoes that started erupting over 70 million years ago, and it still has six active volcanoes today. It's also home to rainforests that are some of the most diverse in the world. If you love surfing, you might know its North Shore, a famous spot called the "Seven Mile Miracle" by surfers. Which state is it?

A) South Carolina
B) Hawaii
C) Florida
D) Rhode Island

111. This state borders Canada and is where you can visit to the International Peace Garden, which sits on the border between both countries. This state is also home to Theodore Roosevelt National Park, where the Great Plains meet the Badlands, and it produces more honey than any other state in the country. Which state is it?
A) Wisconsin
B) Minnesota
C) North Dakota
D) Washington

112. This state borders the Atlantic Ocean and is famous for its blue crabs. Sometimes called "America in Miniature," this state has almost every kind of natural feature you'll find in the U.S., except for a desert. The national anthem, *The Star-Spangled Banner*, was written and inspired by a battle in this state during the War of 1812. It even gave up some land to create Washington, D.C. Which state is it?
A) Virginia
B) Delaware
C) North Carolina
D) Maryland

ANSWERS ON PAGE 107

113. This is the only state named after a U.S. president. It's most famous for its observation tower built for the 1962 World's Fair, called the Space Needle. It's also home to the Olympic, Columbia, and Cascade Mountains, including Mount Rainier and Mount St. Helens, a volcano that had a big eruption in 1980. Plus, this state is where Rainier cherries were first grown. Which state is it?
A) Washington
B) Illinois
C) Virginia
D) Montana

114. This state's name comes from an Algonquin word that means "south wind people," a term used for the Quapaw Native American tribe. It's also where Former President Bill Clinton was born and served as governor. This state played a big role in the fight against school segregation with the Little Rock Nine, who helped make sure all kids, no matter their race, could go to school together. Which state is it?
A) Iowa
B) Arkansas
C) Kentucky
D) Oklahoma

115. This state is where the Declaration of Independence was signed, and it's home to the Liberty Bell, which has the state's name misspelled on it! It also has the most Amish residents in the country, the nation's first zoo, and is where Hershey, the famous chocolate company, was founded and now has its own theme park, Hersheypark. Which state is it?

A) Pennsylvania
B) Louisiana
C) Massachusetts
D) Tennessee

116. This state gets its name from the Spanish word for "colored red" because of its reddish soil. About half of the state is covered by the Rocky Mountains, where you'll find Pike's Peak, the mountain that helped inspire the poem, "America the Beautiful" with its "purple mountain majesties." You can also visit Mesa Verde, where the Ancestral Pueblo people built homes into the cliffs almost a thousand years ago. Which state is it?
A) South Dakota
B) Colorado
C) Wyoming
D) Nevada

117. This state is shaped like a triangle pointing down and was named after King Charles I of England. It borders the Atlantic Ocean and is known for its warm beaches and marshy islands. This state was the first to leave the Union, and the first shots of the Civil War were fired here in 1861. Which state is it?
A) Hawaii
B) Rhode Island
C) South Carolina
D) Florida

ANSWERS ON PAGE 107

118. Even though it doesn't touch the ocean, this state has the largest saltwater lake in the Western Hemisphere, called the Great Salt Lake. It's also home to parts of the Rocky Mountains and the Colorado Plains, as well as Zion and Bryce Canyon National Parks. Plus, it's part of the "Four Corners," the only spot in the U.S. where four states meet. Which state is it?

A) Utah
B) Michigan
C) Colorado
D) Arizona

119. This state is shaped a bit like a heart and shares its name with a river to its south that means "beautiful river" in the Iroquois language. The Wright brothers, who made the first airplane, were from here, and more NASA astronauts have come from this state than any other, including Neil Armstrong, the first person to walk on the moon! You'll also find the Rock and Roll Hall of Fame and the Pro Football Hall of Fame here. Which state is it?

A) Ohio
B) Alabama
C) Colorado
D) Georgia

120. This state was the first U.S. colony to declare independence from Britain, even six months before the Declaration of Independence was signed! It has the shortest coastline of any state touching the ocean and the White Mountains, which are part of the

Appalachian Mountains. (It's no surprise then that skiing is its official state sport!) Which state is it?
A) Maine
B) New Hampshire
C) New Jersey
D) Pennsylvania

121. As the northernmost state in the lower 48 states, this state is where you'll find the Boundary Waters Canoe Area Wilderness, a huge area of wild land that you can explore by canoe. It's also home to the nation's largest shopping mall, which even has an indoor theme park with roller coasters! Which state is it?
A) Minnesota
B) Alaska
C) North Dakota
D) North Carolina

122. This state is famous for its country music. It's where you'll find the Grand Ole Opry, Dollywood (Dolly Parton's theme park), and Elvis Presley's home, Graceland. But it's also known for having the most caves in the country, including the nation's largest underground lake, called The Lost Sea. This state also has the most "horizontal" shape, stretching wide from east to west. Which state is it?
A) Tennessee
B) Wyoming
C) Montana
D) West Virginia

ANSWERS ON PAGE 107

123. This state's name comes from a Sioux word that means "friendly" or "allies." It's where you'll find the largest sculpture in the world, which is why the state is known as "The Mount Rushmore State." But another massive sculpture is being carved here, called the Crazy Horse Memorial. It started in 1948 and will be twice the size of the Statue of Liberty when it's finished, though no one knows when that will be. Which state is it?

A) Kansas
B) Wyoming
C) South Dakota
D) Utah

124. This state is home to Yale University, the house and museum of Mark Twain (who wrote about Tom Sawyer and Huckleberry Finn), the place where the first American dictionary was written by Noah Webster, and the nation's oldest public library. It's also unofficially nicknamed the "Nutmeg State," because early settlers were such clever salespeople that they could even sell fake, wooden nutmegs! Which state is it?

A) Pennsylvania
B) New Jersey
C) Connecticut
D) Vermont

125. This state's name comes from a Sioux word meaning "broad river," referring to the Platte River that runs through it. The Oregon Trail, which pioneers used to travel west, goes through this state. One of the most famous landmarks on the trail is Chimney

Rock, a tall, skinny rock formation in this state that could be seen from miles away. It was such an important marker for pioneers that it's mentioned more than any other landmark in their diaries. Which state is it?

A) Oregon
B) Utah
C) Missouri
D) Nebraska

126. This state, located at the mouth of the Mississippi River and the Gulf of Mexico, is home to the nation's largest river swamp (the Atchafalaya Basin) and the country's largest rose garden, with over 20,000 rosebushes! It's also famous for its Creole and Cajun cultures, being the birthplace of jazz music, and having the biggest Mardi Gras celebration in the country. Which state is it?

A) Texas
B) Louisiana
C) Alabama
D) Mississippi

127. Even though it's the smallest U.S. state (you can drive across it in just 45 minutes!), this state has the longest official name: "State of _____ _____ and Providence Plantations." It was named after a Greek island that was known for religious tolerance, and it's where the first Independence Day celebration in the U.S. took place in 1785. Which state is it?

ANSWERS ON PAGE 107

A) New Jersey
B) North Carolina
C) Connecticut
D) Rhode Island

128. This state, which is square-shaped and landlocked, may have the fewest people in the country, but it's full of natural wonders: It's home to the world's first national park, Yellowstone, where you can see the famous geyser Old Faithful. It also includes parts of the Rocky Mountains, the Great Plains, and the Red Desert, which has the country's largest living sand dune system. This state also produces the most coal. Which state is it?
A) Arizona
B) Wyoming
C) Colorado
D) New Mexico

129. This territory became part of the U.S. after being a Spanish colony for more than 400 years. It's where you'll find the only tropical rainforest in the U.S. National Forest System. In the rainforest, you'll find the kapok, the territory's official tree, which can grow up to 200 feet tall and has stinky-smelling flowers to attract bats for pollination. Which territory is it?
A) Guam
B) Northern Mariana Islands
C) U.S. Virgin Islands
D) Puerto Rico

130. This U.S. territory, known as the "Islands of Paradise," is made up of five volcanic islands and two coral atolls. It has been a part of the U.S. since 1900 after making agreements with local chiefs. Which territory is it?

A) Puerto Rico
B) Northern Mariana Islands
C) American Samoa
D) Guam

ANSWERS ON PAGE 107

GAME #3

RACE THE CLOCK
SOLO CHALLENGE

How many questions can you answer in a set amount of time? Take this challenge to find out!

Number of Players: 1 (solo game)

Instructions:
- The goal in this challenge is to see how many answers you can correctly guess in the given amount of time, so select a category for which you will be answering questions and the amount of time you will give yourself.
- Once you're ready, start the timer and begin recording your answers to the questions in your selected category.
- Continue answering until the timer goes off. Score your answers and make note of how many you got correct.
- Repeat for multiple rounds with new questions, trying to beat your previous score. You can also compare your scores with someone else who's completed this challenge!

STATE NICKNAMES

NATURE-INSPIRED NICKNAMES

131. The state of Washington does not have an official nickname, but one that people often use is based on one of the state's natural features that covers about half the state. What is Washington's common nickname?
A) The Glacier State
B) The Waterfall State
C) The Evergreen State
D) The Mountain State

132. Georgia gets its nickname from one of the prominent crops grown in the state, even though California grows more of this crop. What is Georgia's official nickname?
A) The Cotton State
B) The Pecan State
C) The Peach State
D) The Peanut State

ANSWERS ON PAGE 108

133. Wisconsin gets its nickname from its official state animal, which has long been associated with the state, even though researchers don't even know how many reside in the state! Instead, the state earned this nickname because early miners here worked in environments much like this animal. What is Wisconsin's official nickname?
A) The Groundhog State
B) The Mongoose State
C) The Mole State
D) The Badger State

134. The official nickname for Illinois comes from European settlers who noticed something special about the land of Illinois. What is the official nickname of Illinois?
A) The Prairie State
B) The Fertile State
C) The Springs State
D) The Woodland State

135. Ohio gets its nickname from one of the unique trees that grows naturally here, though the tree's spiky, nut-like seeds are highly toxic if eaten raw. What is Ohio's official nickname?
A) The Pawpaw State
B) The Buckeye State
C) The Beech State
D) The Poplar State

136. Minnesota does not have an official nickname, however one of its most common ones (which also appears on its license plates) refers to its large concentration—more than 11,000!—of one particular geologic feature found throughout the state. What is Minnesota's nickname?
A) Land of 10,000 Lakes
B) Land of 10,000 Meadows
C) Land of 10,000 Caves
D) Land of 10,000 Rivers

137. Oregon is named after its official state animal, which served a prominent role in the state's fur-trade history, especially for making fur hats. Though the animal is no longer hunted, it still serves an important role in shaping the state's natural environment. What is Oregon's official nickname?
A) The Fox State
B) The Mink State
C) The Racoon State
D) The Beaver State

138. Kentucky gets its state nickname from a plant grown here to feed the thoroughbred race horses the state is famous for. What is Kentucky's official nickname?
A) The Bluegrass State
B) The Fescue State
C) The Alfalfa State
D) The Rye State

ANSWERS ON PAGE 108

139. Mississippi gets its nickname from its state tree, which remains evergreen and whose large, white flowers bloom throughout May and June. What is Mississippi's official nickname?

A) The Redbud State
B) The Cypress State
C) The Holly State
D) The Magnolia State

140. Vermont gets its nickname from a mountain range found in the state, which is part of the Appalachians. What is Vermont's nickname?

A) The Hudson Highlands State
B) The Adirondack Mountain State
C) The Green Mountain State
D) The White Mountains State

141. Michigan has many nicknames—including the "Great Lakes State," printed on its license plates. However, its most traditional nickname comes from an animal that's not very common in Michigan. In fact, the first time this animal was seen in over 200 years was in 2004! Some people think Michigan got this nickname because the state helped move these animals during the fur trade. Others say it's because the people of Michigan are like this animal. What is Michigan's traditional nickname?

A) The Lynx State
B) The Badger State
C) The Wolverine State
D) The Polar Bear State

ARE YOU HAVING FUN LEARNING ABOUT THE UNITED STATES?!

LEAVE A REVIEW!
THEY REALLY HELP!

142. Rhode Island selected its official nickname to attract tourists by appealing to its location on the Atlantic Ocean. What is Rhode Island's official nickname?

A) Coastline State
B) Sailing State
C) Island State
D) Ocean State

143. South Carolina gets its nickname from its state tree, which also appears on its state flag and seal. Native to the Southeastern United States, the fan-leafed tree can grow up to 60 feet tall, withstand high winds, and live for more than 200 years. What is South Carolina's official nickname?

A) The Pine State
B) The Palmetto State
C) The Cedar State
D) The Willow State

144. Florida's official nickname was inspired by the state's weather. What is Florida's official nickname?

A) The Hurricane State
B) The Sunshine State
C) The Tropical State
D) The Summer State

145. West Virginia gets its nickname from one of the state's natural features, which stretches across almost the entire state. What is West Virginia's nickname?

A) The River State
B) The Cave State

C) The Coal State
D) The Mountain State

146. North Dakota does not have an official nickname, but one of its most common ones is as "The Flickertail State," which refers to an animal commonly found here that is known for "flicking" its tail. What kind of animal is a "flickertail"?
A) Meadowlark
B) Ground squirrel
C) Deer
D) Bobcat

147. Massachusetts has a nickname that comes from something special about its land, as a coastal state along the Atlantic Ocean. Which of the following is one of its nicknames?
A) Cape State
B) Bay State
C) Whale-Watching State
D) Sand Dune State

148. New Hampshire does not have an official nickname, but a common one comes from a natural resource found in the state's bedrock and is used in building. Which of the following is New Hampshire's state nickname?
A) Garnet State
B) Granite State
C) Sandstone State
D) Quartz State

ANSWERS ON PAGES 108

149. Louisiana's official nickname comes from its state bird. In the 1800s, this water bird almost disappeared because people hunted it for its feathers to make hats. Now, the bird's population has grown, so it's no longer endangered. What is Louisiana's official nickname?

A) Loon State

B) Spoonbill State

C) Pelican State

D) Egret State

150. California's official nickname comes from both the state flower (the California poppy), as well as one of the state's natural resources that made the state famous in the 1800s. What is California's official nickname?

A) Golden State

B) Redwood State

C) Pacific Paradise

D) Sunshine State

151. Nevada doesn't have an official nickname, but it's often called by a name that comes from something valuable found in the state during the 1800s. Even today, Nevada produces more of this material than any other state. What is Nevada's most popular nickname?

A) Copper State

B) Mercury State

C) Lithium State

D) Silver State

152. The official nickname for Kansas comes from a flower that grows naturally throughout the state and is also the state flower for Kansas. What is Kansas's official nickname?
A) Milkweed State
B) Coneflower State
C) Bluebell State
D) Sunflower State

153. Idaho's official nickname comes from the large number of minerals found in the state—more than 200 different kinds! What is Idaho's official nickname?
A) Mineral State
B) Rock State
C) Gem State
D) Crystal State

154. Arizona's official nickname comes from one of the state's main natural attractions. What is Arizona's official nickname?
A) Monument Valley State
B) Grand Canyon State
C) Camelback Mountain State
D) Lake Powell State

155. Maine has two official nicknames. One is Vacationland, which appears on license plates. The other reflects the fact that Maine's forests cover more than 80 percent of its land, making it the most forested state in the U.S. What is Maine's second official nickname?

ANSWERS ON PAGE 108

A) Pine Tree State
B) Birch Tree State
C) Beech Tree State
D) Elm Tree

156. Montana does not have an official state nickname, but a common one refers to the state's valuable natural resources. What is this nickname for Montana?
A) The Treasure State
B) The Gold State
C) The Sapphire State
D) The Gemstone State

HISTORICAL NICKNAMES

157. In 1639, Connecticut wrote and adopted a document called the Fundamental Orders. It is considered to be one of the first written documents of its kind and inspired the state's nickname. What is Connecticut's official nickname?
A) The Constitution State
B) The Declaration State
C) The Independence State
D) The Legislation State

158. South Dakota's nickname comes from a massive monument here, completed in 1941. What is South Dakota's official nickname?
A) The Wind Cave State
B) The Crazy Horse Memorial State

C) The Badlands State
D) The Mount Rushmore State

159. Delaware's official nickname refers to the fact that it was the first state to ratify the Constitution in 1787 as one of the 13 original states. What is Delaware's official nickname?
A) The Key State
B) The Original State
C) The First State
D) The Pioneer State

160. Colorado got its nickname because it became the 38th U.S. state in 1876, exactly 100 years after the Declaration of Independence was signed. What is Colorado's nickname?
A) Independence State
B) Freedom State
C) Centennial State
D) Signature State

161. Pennsylvania is the state where both the Declaration of Independence and Constitution were written, and its nickname reflects how important the state was in the founding of the United States. What is Pennsylvania's nickname?
A) Keystone State
B) Pivotal State
C) Essential State
D) Monumental State

ANSWERS ON PAGE 108

162. Virginia was the first of the 13 original colonies of England, from which it gets one of its main nicknames. Which of the following is one of Virginia's nicknames?
A) Old Dominion
B) The Original
C) The First Colony
D) Proud Province

163. George Washington gave Maryland one of its oldest nicknames, which comes from when Maryland soldiers helped save the Continental Army during an important battle in the American Revolution. What is Maryland's nickname?
A) State of Valor
B) Mighty State
C) Old Line State
D) Guardian State

164. People aren't sure where Iowa's nickname came from. Some think it was named after a local Native American chief, while others think it was inspired by a character from the book, *The Last of the Mohicans*. Either way, by 1840, Iowans had embraced the nickname. What is Iowa's nickname?
A) The Chingachgook State
B) The Heyward State
C) The Magua State
D) The Hawkeye State

165. During the Civil War, the capital of the Confederacy was located in Alabama, which inspired one of its unofficial nicknames. What of the following is Alabama's nickname?
A) Southern Pride
B) The Heart of Dixie
C) State of the South
D) Dixie Land

166. Oklahoma's unofficial nickname is "The Sooner State," which comes from when people rushed to claim land there "sooner" than they were supposed to in the 1800s. But the state's official nickname, used on license plates, reflects the large number of Native Americans who live here. (It's where you'll find both the Cherokee and Choctaw Nation Reservations.) What is the official nickname for Oklahoma?
A) Native America
B) National Reserves
C) The First Peoples State
D) The Original State

167. Tennessee's nickname (used on license plates) comes from the willingness of Tennesseans to serve during important wars, including the War of 1812 and the Mexican-American War in the late 1840s. What is Tennessee's nickname?
A) State of Service
B) Soldier State
C) Brave State
D) Volunteer State

ANSWERS ON PAGE 108

168. Wyoming has three official nicknames: One is "Big Wyoming," because of the state's size. Another is "Cowboy State," because of its ranching history. The third nickname is because Wyoming was the first state in the country to give women the right to vote. What is this third official nickname for Wyoming?

A) Justice State
B) Voting State
C) Equality State
D) Freedom State

169. Texas was its own independent country for almost ten years before it joined the United States in 1845. This is what inspired Texas's official nickname. Which of the following is it?

A) Lone Star State
B) Republic State
C) State of Independence
D) Liberty State

170. Guam's nickname refers to the people who archaeologists believe have lived on the island since 1500 BC. What is Guam's nickname?

A) Land of the Chamorro
B) Polynesian Paradise
C) Discover the Tokelau
D) Palauan Enchantment

OTHER NICKNAMES
(INSPIRED BY STATE INDUSTRY, PEOPLE, ETC.)

171. New Jersey's official nickname (found on state license plates) is about how the state was known for growing food and vegetables for nearby states during the 1800s. What is New Jersey's nickname?
A) Orchard State
B) Garden State
C) Farmstead State
D) Bushel State

172. Alaska's official nickname comes from the fact that much of the state is still largely unexplored. What is Alaska's official nickname?
A) Last Frontier
B) Vast Possibilities
C) Beyond Boundaries
D) Wanderer State

173. New Mexico got its nickname from the title of a book written in 1906 about the state. What is New Mexico's official nickname?
A) Unforgettable Treasures
B) Gateway to the Southwest
C) Sunset State
D) Land of Enchantment

174. Arkansas's official nickname comes from the state's natural beauty. It was chosen to attract tourists to come visit. What is Arkansas's official nickname?

ANSWERS ON PAGE 108

A) Ozark State
B) Natural State
C) Scenic State
D) Wilderness State

175. North Carolina has lots of pine forests, which it can use to make things like rosin, tar, and oil. One of its popular nicknames is believed to come from this. What is North Carolina's popular nickname?
A) Turpentine State
B) Rosin State
C) Tar Heel State
D) Pine Oil State

176. Missouri's nickname, which you can see on license plates, comes from a saying that means people from Missouri need to see something before they believe it. What is Missouri's nickname?
A) Skeptical State
B) Show Me State
C) See It, Believe It State
D) Possibilities State

177. Utah's state motto is, "Industry," because people who live there are known as hard workers. The state nickname comes from a symbol used on the state flag, seal and emblem that stands for this kind of hard work. What is Utah's unofficial nickname?
A) Ant State
B) Beehive State
C) Horse State
D) Cattle State

178. Nebraska's official nickname comes from the mascot for one of the state's athletic university teams. What is Nebraska's official nickname?

A) Wildcat State

B) Mavericks State

C) Durango State

D) Cornhusker State

179. Hawaii gets its official nickname from a traditional Polynesian greeting used on the islands. What is Hawaii's official nickname?

A) Owhyhee State

B) Aloha State

C) Ohana State

D) Hula State

180. Even when the U.S. was a young country, New York was an important state. That's where its nickname comes from—which even George Washington used to describe New York! What is New York's state nickname?

A) Vitality State

B) Prominence State

C) Empire State

D) Mushroom State

181. Indiana does not have an official nickname, but its most popular nickname comes from a word used to describe people from the state. Some people think this word came from a poem; a last name; or what people would say when visiting someone's home. What is Indiana's unofficial nickname?

ANSWERS ON PAGE 108

A) Hoosier State
B) Pioneer State
C) Wabash State
D) Eerie State

GAME #4

TIMER HOT SEAT CHALLENGE

How many questions can players correctly answer in a set amount of time? This challenge will put them to the test!

Number of Players: 2 or more

Instructions:
- Determine which category you will read questions from, and which player will go first.
- That player will select 10 questions in sequential order to ask, and write down the answers to those questions before the round begins.
- Another player will be chosen to be in the "Hot Seat" and must answer the selected questions as quickly as possible.
- When the round begins, start a timer.
- If the player answers correctly, the asking player will move on to the next question. However, if the answer is incorrect, the asking player will inform they are wrong and the player in the "Hot Seat" must guess again until they get the correct answer.
- Once the player has answered all 10 questions correctly, stop the timer and record the time.
- Change roles, and repeat until all players have had a chance in the "Hot Seat." The winner is the player or team with the lowest time.

STATE SYMBOLS

STATE ANIMALS

182. The marmot is a large rodent related to squirrels that can be found around the world. However, the Olympic marmot (about the size of a house cat with a long, bushy tail) can only be found in this state. Which state named the Olympic marmot as its state animal?
A) Vermont
B) MInnesota
C) Washington
D) Michigan

183. The grey fox has lived in this state for millions of years and is the only dog-like animal that can climb trees! It doesn't hibernate, which inspired students to ask the government to make it the state animal because it's "always ready." Which state named the grey fox its state animal?
A) Maine
B) Alaska
C) North Carolina
D) Delaware

184. The right whale is one of the most endangered whales in the world, with only about 350 left! These whales come back to the coast of this state to have their babies, which makes all North right whales native only to this state. Massachusetts named the right whale as its state animal, but this state named the right whale its state marine mammal. Which state is it?
A) Georgia
B) Florida
C) Louisiana
D) Hawaii

185. The _____ panther, named after this state, can grow up to six feet long and is pale brown. Even though it's been illegal to hunt them since 1958, this panther is still endangered, with only about 120 to 230 adult panthers left because they're losing their natural homes. Which state named the _____ panther its state animal?
A) South Carolina
B) Florida
C) Arizona
D) Georgia

186. Named after this state, the _____ mules are a special kind of mule—a mix between a female horse and a male donkey. They are known for being super strong and tough, perfect for pulling pioneer wagons in this state, which named them its state animal in 1995. Which state named the _____ mule its state animal?

ANSWERS ON PAGE 109

A) Missouri
B) Nebraska
C) Kentucky
D) Iowa

187. Grizzly bears can only be found in five U.S. states —including this one, where they live in Glacier National Park, located in this state. (Don't mix them up with the California grizzly bear, which is the state animal of California but is now extinct due to hunting.) Which state named the grizzly bear its state animal?
A) Alaska
B) North Dakota
C) Ohio
D) Montana

188. The desert bighorn sheep can survive for days without water, sometimes breaking open cacti with their horns to drink! Their hooves help them live in the desert mountains of this state, where they're from. Which state named the desert bighorn its state animal?
A) New Mexico
B) Arizona
C) Nevada
D) Texas

189. Along with the bald eagle, the American bison is the national animal for the U.S. It is also the state animal of three states, including Wyoming, Oklahoma and this state, which was home to Charles "Buffalo"

Jones who helped save the bison from almost disappearing in the 1870s. Which state (besides Wyoming and Oklahoma) also named the American bison its state animal?
A) Kansas
B) Colorado
C) North Dakota
D) Arkansas

190. The Nokota horse is a wild horse breed that comes from Sioux Chief Sitting Bull's war ponies. Some of these horses still run free in Theodore Roosevelt National Park and the Badlands of this state. Which state named the Nokota horse as its state horse?
A) Oklahoma
B) North Dakota
C) Arkansas
D) Nebraska

191. This state catches the most lobsters of any state, even though they are found all along the Atlantic Coast. Which state named the American lobster its state crustacean?
A) New York
B) Connecticut
C) Maryland
D) Maine

192. Named after this state, the _____ cave salamander lives in caves and is a big salamander with red gills, small eyes, and a fin on its tail. Which state

ANSWERS ON PAGE 109

named the _____ cave salamander as its state amphibian?
A) Tennessee
B) Kentucky
C) Alabama
D) Georgia

193. Moose are found in the Northern United States where it's cold and there are lots of forests near fresh water. While Maine also has the moose as its state animal, the biggest number of moose are found in this state. Which state, besides Maine, named the moose as its state animal?
A) Michigan
B) Oregon
C) Alaska
D) New Hampshire

194. The big brown bat became the official animal of this U.S. territory or district in 2020. It is still found here, even though it has faced challenges like habitat loss and a sickness called white-nose syndrome. Which U.S. territory or district has the big brown bat as its official state animal?
A) Northern Mariana Islands
B) Washington, D.C.
C) U.S. Virgin Islands
D) Puerto Rico

195. The coqui is a small frog found in this U.S. territory or district and gets its name from the sound it makes at night, "ko-kee." An old story says that a

goddess made the frog to call out the name of her lost love, Coqui. Which U.S. territory or district has the coqui as its official animal?

A) Guam

B) Washington, D.C.

C) U.S. Virgin Islands

D) Puerto Rico

196. While a few states share the same state animal, there is one animal that is shared the most. It is the same state animal for all the following states: Arkansas, Georgia, Illinois, Michigan, Mississippi, Nebraska, New Hampshire, Ohio, Pennsylvania, and South Carolina. Which animal is it?

A) Bald eagle

B) Red fox

C) Gray squirrel

D) White-tailed deer

STATE BIRDS

197. The scissor-tailed flycatcher has tail feathers that spread open and close like scissors when it flies. This bird likes open prairies and to build its nests in this state. Which state has named the scissor-tailed flycatcher its state bird?

A) Kansas

B) Oklahoma

C) Arkansas

D) Iowa

ANSWERS ON PAGE 109

198. The purple finch is a bird that gets its name from the reddish-purple color seen on males. This bird was once kept in cages because it sings so beautifully. Which state has named the purple finch its state bird?

A) New Jersey
B) New Hampshire
C) New York
D) Rhode Island

199. Even though its name is the California gull, it isn't the state bird of California. Instead, it is the state bird of a different state where the gulls were seen as an answer to prayer: They helped save pioneer farmers' crops by eating the insects that were ruining their fields. Which state named the California gull its state bird?

A) Oregon
B) Idaho
C) South Dakota
D) Utah

200. The nēnē is the rarest goose in the world and is currently endangered. It is believed to have evolved from the Canada goose and is found only in this state. Which state named the nēnē its state bird?

A) Washington
B) Arizona
C) Hawaii
D) Florida

201. The Baltimore oriole has orange and black feathers—the same colors as the crest for the Baltimore family, who settled in this state. Which state named the Baltimore oriole as its state bird?
A) Maryland
B) Massachusetts
C) Michigan
D) Missouri

202. The common loon—which looks like a duck but is not—lives entirely on water unless it is nesting. This state is where more loons nest than in any other contiguous state. Which state named the common loon its state bird?
A) Washington
B) Wisconsin
C) New Jersey
D) Minnesota

203. Named for the state where this bird was developed in the late 1800s, the _____ _____ Red is a chicken raised for its meat and egg-laying abilities. What state named the _____ _____ Red its state bird?
A) Maine
B) Rhode Island
C) New Jersey
D) Delaware

204. This bird is called the ko'ko and is found only on this U.S. territory. For almost 40 years after World War II, it was extinct in the wild. But in 2019, it was successfully brought back into the wild, and is only

ANSWERS ON PAGE 109

the second bird in history that has been able to recover from extinction in the wild. Which U.S. territory has the ko'ko as its national bird?

A) Guam

B) American Samoa

C) Northern Mariana Islands

D) Puerto Rico

205. The bananaquit is a small songbird that loves ripe bananas and has a yellow belly. Which U.S. territory or district has named the bananaquit its official bird?

A) Northern Mariana Islands

B) Washington, D.C.

C) U.S. Virgin Islands

D) Puerto Rico

206. Named after the U.S. territory where it lives, the _____ fruit dove is a colorful dove with green, red, and yellow spots. It's only found on a few islands in the Pacific Ocean. Which U.S. territory named the _____ fruit dove its official bird?

A) U.S. Virgin Islands

B) American Samoa

C) Puerto Rico

D) Northern Mariana Islands

207. Many states choose the same bird to represent them, but one bird is the most popular. It is the state bird for seven different states, including Kentucky, Illinois, Indiana, Ohio, Virginia, North Carolina, and West Virginia. Which state bird is it?

A) Northern cardinal
B) American robin
C) Northern mockingbird
D) Eastern bluebird

STATE FLOWERS

208. Known for its bright blue flowers, bluebonnets only grow in this state, where they are also celebrated during a state-wide festival. Which state named the bluebonnet its state flower?
A) **Minnesota**
B) Louisiana
C) Washington
D) Texas

209. Named after this state, the _____ blue columbine is a special flower that only grows high up in the Rocky Mountains. Because it's so rare, the flower is protected by law so people don't pick it. Which state named the _____ blue columbine its state flower?
A) Colorado
B) Idaho
C) Montana
D) Wyoming

210. The Saguaro cactus is only found in the Sonoran Desert, and its flowers (which bloom in late spring with white flowers) are the state flower for which state?

ANSWERS ON PAGE 109

A) California
B) New Mexico
C) Arizona
D) Nevada

211. Mountain laurel is found all over the Eastern U.S., and it's the state flower of both Pennsylvania and this state. It has beautiful pink and white blossoms and can even grow in rocky mountain soil. This represents the strength of the people in this state. Which state (besides Pennsylvania) has mountain laurel as its state flower?
A) Ohio
B) Virginia
C) Connecticut
D) Tennessee

212. In Washington, a type of Rhododendron called "Coast rhododendron" is the state flower. But in this state, the "Great rhododendron" was chosen as the state flower by students because it is found throughout the state in its wet woods. Which state voted rhododendron as its state flower?
A) West Virginia
B) Massachusetts
C) Ohio
D) North Carolina

213. The magnolia flower is the state flower of Louisiana, and it's also the state flower *and* state tree of this state. Which state named the magnolia as both its state flower and state tree?

A) West Virginia
B) Mississippi
C) Missouri
D) Oklahoma

214. The apple blossom is the state flower for Arkansas and also for this state, which is the third-largest apple producer in the country. Which state (besides Arkansas) has the apple blossom as its state flower?
A) Montana
B) Michigan
C) Iowa
D) Tennessee

215. The mayflower is a trailing evergreen shrub with pink and white flowers that has been on the endangered list since 1925. This state chose it as its state flower because it's also the state where the Pilgrims' Mayflower ship landed In 1620. Which state named the mayflower its state flower?
A) Virginia
B) Connecticut
C) Massachusetts
D) Delaware

216. The yellow trumpetbush, also known as ginger Thomas, is the official flower and tree of this U.S. territory or district, even though it's not originally from here. It's celebrated for its bright yellow flowers and its leaves have been used as natural remedies.

ANSWERS ON PAGE 109

Which U.S. territory or district named the yellow trumpetbush as its official flower and tree?
A) Northern Mariana Islands
B) Washington, D.C.
C) American Samoa
D) U.S. Virgin Islands

217. Several states have the same state flower, but one flower is the most popular. It is the state flower for Georgia, Iowa, North Dakota, New York, Oklahoma, and Washington D.C. Which flower is it?
A) Tulip
B) Lilac
C) Daisy
D) Rose

STATE TREES

218. The Eastern hemlock tree was used during pioneer times to build cabins in this state, where it grows naturally. But by the 1900s, it had been cut down so much that it was becoming rare, so this state chose the Eastern hemlock as its state tree to help protect it for the future. (It's different from the Western hemlock, which Washington named its state tree.) Which state named the Eastern hemlock its state tree?
A) Pennsylvania
B) Virginia
C) Maryland
D) Indiana

219. The longleaf pine can grow over 100 feet tall and can survive fires, floods, droughts, and hurricanes. Unfortunately, only about three percent of these trees are left because so many have been cut down. Which state chose the longleaf pine as its state tree to help raise awareness about this endangered tree?
A) Oklahoma
B) Texas
C) North Carolina
D) Alabama

220. The white oak tree can live for 350 to 500 years and grows across eastern and central North America. It is found in all 102 counties of this state, which named it its state tree. Which state is it?
A) New Hampshire
B) Illinois
C) Tennessee
D) Wisconsin

221. The bald cypress tree lives in swamps and wet areas of this state. It's called the "wood eternal" because it doesn't decay easily, which makes it useful for building. It's even used to build wooden boats, called pirogues. Which state named the bald cypress its state tree?
A) Florida
B) Alabama
C) Mississippi
D) Louisiana

ANSWERS ON PAGE 109

222. The Douglas fir (which is not a true fir tree) is an evergreen tree found throughout western North America, including this state. Which state named the Douglas fir its state tree?
A) Wyoming
B) North Dakota
C) Oregon
D) Idaho

223. The flowering dogwood tree is known for its large, beautiful flowers (usually white and green but sometimes pink) that bloom during the spring. This tree is both the state flower and the state tree of one state. (It is also the state flower—but not the state tree—of North Carolina, and the state tree—but not the state flower—of Missouri.) Which state named the flowering dogwood both its state flower and state tree?
A) Virginia
B) Pennsylvania
C) Indiana
D) New York

224. This state picked two types of redwood trees as its state trees. Both grow naturally in this state and have been around since the time of dinosaurs: The Coast redwood is the tallest tree in the world and can live for 2,000 years, while the giant Sequoia is the largest tree by volume and can live for about 3,000 years. Which state named both the Coast redwood and the giant Sequoia as its state trees?

A) Hawaii
B) California
C) Utah
D) Wyoming

225. Cottonwood trees are large and shady, known for the fluffy white "cotton" that carries their seeds. They grow quickly and provide most of the lumber in this state, which named the cottonwood as its state tree. Which state is it?
A) Nebraska
B) Alabama
C) South Carolina
D) Kansas

226. The hala tree, also known as the paogo, grows near the ocean in this U.S. territory or district. This tree bears a fruit that looks like a pineapple that some have said looks like "an exploding planet." Which territory or district named the hala tree its official tree?
A) Northern Mariana Islands
B) Washington, D.C.
C) American Samoa
D) U.S. Virgin Islands

227. The flame tree, with its bright red flowers that look like flames, is originally from Madagascar (more than 7,000 miles away) but now is grown in this U.S. territory. Which U.S. territory named the flame tree its official tree?

ANSWERS ON PAGE 109

A) American Samoa
B) Northern Mariana Islands
C) Puerto Rico
D) Guam

STATE GEMSTONES, MINERALS & ROCKS

228. Turquoise is a green-blue gemstone found in the Southwest, where it was considered sacred to Indigenous communities. It's also the state gemstone of Arizona, but in this state, you'll find the Turquoise Museum and some of the oldest turquoise mines in the U.S. Which state (besides Arizona) named turquoise its state gemstone?
A) Texas
B) New Mexico
C) California
D) Nevada

229. Freshwater pearls used to be found all over this state, but the mussels that produce them have become rare. Now, most freshwater pearls are produced in nearby Tennessee, which has named the Tennessee River pearl its state gemstone. Which other state (besides Tennessee) named freshwater pearls its state gemstone?
A) Mississippi
B) Kentucky
C) West Virginia
D) Pennsylvania

230. Geodes are round rocks that are hollow inside and filled with crystals. You can find them in deserts, stream beds, and places with volcanic ash or limestone. This state is one of the best places in the U.S. to find geodes. Which state named geodes its official state rock?
A) California
B) Montana
C) Iowa
D) Hawaii

231. Star garnets are usually dark purple or plum-colored garnets that have a natural star-shaped reflection on their surface. They are so rare that there are only two places in the world where they are found: India and this state. Which state named the star garnet its state gemstone?
A) New Hampshire
B) Wisconsin
C) Indiana
D) Idaho

232. Jade is found in this state as well as in Alaska, which also named jade its state gemstone. But the jade from this state is famous for its bright, apple-green color and is considered some of the best and most valuable jade in the world. Which state (besides Alaska) named jade its state gemstone?
A) Wyoming
B) Rhode Island
C) Connecticut
D) Colorado

ANSWERS ON PAGE 109

233. While most diamonds today come from other countries, diamonds have been found in the United States. The largest U.S. diamond ever found is called the "Uncle Sam" and was found in this state. Which state named the diamond its state gemstone?
A) Delaware
B) Missouri
C) Arkansas
D) Vermont

234. Garnets are known for their deep red color and can be found in the U.S., including Connecticut (which named garnet its state gemstone). But this state is home to the largest garnet mine in the world, located in its Adirondack Mountains. Which state (besides Connecticut) named the garnet its state gemstone?
A) South Dakota
B) New York
C) Nevada
D) Maine

235. Emeralds are prized for their rich green color and considered one of the "big four" gemstones, along with diamonds, rubies, and sapphires. The only significant emerald deposits in North America are found in this state. Which state named the emerald its state gemstone?
A) Rhode Island
B) Illinois
C) Vermont
D) North Carolina

236. Amethyst is a purple gemstone that can be found across the U.S. However, some of the best-quality amethysts were discovered in this state and are now displayed in museums like the Smithsonian Museum of Natural History. Which state named the amethyst its state gemstone?
A) South Carolina
B) West Virginia
C) Oregon
D) Nebraska

237. Granite is a common rock made from different minerals, often used for building. One rare type of granite is red granite, which can be found in this state. Which state named red granite its state rock?
A) Georgia
B) Utah
C) Wisconsin
D) Minnesota

238. Potomac bluestone is the official rock of this U.S. territory or district where it can be found. It was used to build many of the important buildings here, including the U.S. Capitol and White House. Which U.S. territory or district named Potomac bluestone its official rock?
A) Northern Mariana Islands
B) Washington, D.C.
C) U.S. Virgin Islands
D) Puerto Rico

ANSWERS ON PAGE 109

STATE FOSSILS

239. When railroad workers were digging the first railroad across this state, they found the skeleton of a large beluga whale—about 200 miles away from the nearest ocean! This kind of whale is still around today, which makes it the only state fossil to belong to a living species. Which state named the beluga whale its state fossil?
A) Utah
B) Vermont
C) Louisiana
D) Alaska

240. The *Hadrosaurus foulkii* was the first nearly complete dinosaur skeleton found in North America. This duck-billed dinosaur skeleton was found in a marl pit in this state in 1858. Which state named the *Hadrosaurus foulkii* its state fossil?
A) Illinois
B) South Dakota
C) Delaware
D) New Jersey

241. The *Triceratops* is famous for its three horns and has been found in many places, including in this state where a nearly complete *Triceratops* skull was unearthed. Which state named the *Triceratops* its state fossil?
A) New Mexico
B) Mississippi
C) South Dakota
D) Kansas

242. The American mastodon is a smaller cousin of the woolly mammoth and has been found in many states (including Michigan, which also named it as its state fossil). Mastodon remains have been found in every county of this state, and it is the state's most common ice age fossil. Which state (besides Michigan) named the American mastodon its state fossil?
A) Pennsylvania
B) Illinois
C) Indiana
D) Kentucky

243. Trilobites were ancient sea creatures with hard shells, similar to today's horseshoe crabs. They lived in the ocean long before the dinosaurs during a time when much of this state was covered by a shallow sea. (Wisconsin and Pennsylvania also named the trilobite their state fossil.) Which state (besides Wisconsin and Pennsylvania) named the trilobite its state fossil?
A) Ohio
B) Maryland
C) South Carolina
D) Colorado

ANSWERS ON PAGE 109

GAME #5

TRIVIA TITAN CHALLENGE

Who really knows their stuff? The only way to find out is to put them to the test—without any multiple-choice answers! Instead, players must rely on their knowledge to answer correctly.

Number of Players: 2 or more (individually or as teams)

Instructions:
- Determine which category you will use.
- One player will read the question and another player will answer. Determine which players will start in each of those roles.
- The player asking the question will select a question to read but will *not* read the answers.
- The answering player must come up with the answer based on their already-existing knowledge. If desired, use a timer.
- If they get the answer correct, they earn one point. If not, no points are awarded. Keep score.
- Switch roles, and ask a new question.
- Continue until all players have gone an equal amount of times. The winner with the most points at the end of the game is crowned "Trivia Titan!"

HAVE EVEN MORE TRIVIA FUN!

LEARN ALL ABOUT YOUR FAVORITE HOLIDAYS!

MAKE LEARNING ABOUT SCIENCE FEEL LIKE A GAME!

STATE CAPITALS

Alabama: Montgomery
Alaska: Juneau
Arizona: Phoenix
Arkansas: Little Rock
California: Sacramento
Colorado: Denver
Connecticut: Hartford
Delaware: Dover
Florida: Tallahassee
Georgia: Atlanta
Hawaii: Honolulu
Idaho: Boise
Illinois: Springfield
Indiana: Indianapolis
Iowa: Des Moines
Kansas: Topeka
Kentucky: Frankfort
Louisiana: Baton Rouge
Maine: Augusta
Maryland: Annapolis
Massachusetts: Boston
Michigan: Lansing
Minnesota: Saint Paul
Mississippi: Jackson
Missouri: Jefferson City
Montana: Helena
Nebraska: Lincoln
Nevada: Carson City
New Hampshire: Concord

New Jersey: Trenton
New Mexico: Santa Fe
New York: Albany
North Carolina: Raleigh
North Dakota: Bismarck
Ohio: Columbus
Oklahoma: Oklahoma City
Oregon: Salem
Pennsylvania: Harrisburg
Rhode Island: Providence
South Carolina: Columbia
South Dakota: Pierre
Tennessee: Nashville
Texas: Austin
Utah: Salt Lake City
Vermont: Montpelier
Virginia: Richmond
Washington: Olympia
West Virginia: Charleston
Wisconsin: Madison
Wyoming: Cheyenne

U.S. TERRITORIES
American Samoa: Pago Pago
Guam: Hagåtña
Northern Mariana Islands: Saipan
Puerto Rico: San Juan
U.S. Virgin Islands: Charlotte Amalie

STATE NICKNAMES

Alabama: The Heart of Dixie *
Alaska: Last Frontier
Arizona: Grand Canyon State
Arkansas: Natural State
California: Golden State
Colorado: Centennial State
Connecticut: The Constitution State
Delaware: The First State
Florida: The Sunshine State
Georgia: The Peach State
Hawaii: Aloha State
Idaho: Gem State
Illinois: The Prairie State
Indiana: Hoosier State *
Iowa: The Hawkeye State
Kansas: Sunflower State
Kentucky: The Bluegrass State
Louisiana: Pelican State
Maine: Pine Tree State
Maryland: Old Line State *
Massachusetts: Bay State *
Michigan: The Wolverine State *
Minnesota: Land of 10,000 Lakes *
Mississippi: The Magnolia State
Missouri: Show Me State *
Montana: The Treasure State *
Nebraska: Cornhusker State
Nevada: The Silver State *
New Hampshire: Granite State *
New Jersey: Garden State
New Mexico: Land of Enchantment

New York: Empire State
North Carolina: Tar Heel State *
North Dakota: The Flickertail State *
Ohio: The Buckeye State
Oklahoma: Native America
Oregon: The Beaver State
Pennsylvania: Keystone State
Rhode Island: Ocean State
South Carolina: The Palmetto State
South Dakota: The Mount Rushmore State
Tennessee: Volunteer State
Texas: Lone Star State
Utah: Beehive State *
Vermont: The Green Mountain State
Virginia: Old Dominion
Washington: The Evergreen State *
West Virginia: The Mountain State
Wisconsin: The Badger State
Wyoming: The Equality State

U.S. DISTRICT & TERRITORIES

Washington D.C.: Nation's Capital
Puerto Rico: Island of Enchantment
Guam: Land of the Chamorro
American Samoa: Islands of Paradise
U.S. Virgin Islands: America's Paradise *
Northern Mariana Islands: None

* Unofficial nicknames

STATE ANIMALS

Alabama: Black bear
Alaska: Moose
Arizona: Ringtail
Arkansas: White-tailed deer
California: California grizzly bear
Colorado: Rocky Mountain bighorn sheep
Connecticut: Sperm whale
Delaware: Grey fox
Florida: Florida panther
Georgia: White-tailed deer
Hawaii: Hawaiian monk seal
Idaho: Appaloosa horse
Illinois: White-tailed deer
Indiana: None
Iowa: None
Kansas: American bison
Kentucky: Thoroughbred (horse)
Louisiana: Black bear
Maine: Moose
Maryland: Thoroughbred (horse)
Massachusetts: Right whale (marine mammal)
Michigan: White-tailed deer
Minnesota: None
Mississippi: White-tailed deer
Missouri: Missouri mule
Montana: Grizzly bear
Nebraska: White-tailed deer
Nevada: Desert bighorn sheep
New Hampshire: White-tailed deer
New Jersey: Horse

New Mexico: American black bear
New York: Beaver
North Carolina: Eastern gray squirrel
North Dakota: Nokota horse (horse)
Ohio: White-tailed deer
Oklahoma: American bison
Oregon: American beaver
Pennsylvania: White-tailed deer
Rhode Island: Harbor seal (marine mammal)
South Carolina: White-tailed deer
South Dakota: Coyote
Tennessee: Raccoon
Texas: Nine-banded armadillo (small mammal)
Utah: None
Vermont: Morgan horse
Virginia: American foxhound (dog)
Washington: Olympic marmot (endemic mammal)
West Virginia: Black bear
Wisconsin: Badger
Wyoming: American bison

U.S. DISTRICT & TERRITORIES
Washington D.C.: Big brown bat
American Samoa: None
Guam: None
Northern Mariana Islands: None
Puerto Rico: Coqui frog
U.S. Virgin Islands: None

(Unless otherwise stated, state animals or mammals are listed. Some states designate various state animals, including amphibians, crustaceans, horses, dogs, cats, etc., which are not all listed here.)

STATE BIRDS

Alabama: Yellowhammer
Alaska: Willow ptarmigan
Arizona: Cactus wren
Arkansas: Northern mockingbird
California: California quail
Colorado: Lark bunting
Connecticut: American robin
Delaware: Delaware Blue hen
Florida: Northern mockingbird
Georgia: Brown thrasher
Hawaii: Nēnē (Hawaiian goose)
Idaho: Mountain bluebird
Illinois: Northern cardinal
Indiana: Northern cardinal
Iowa: Eastern goldfinch
Kansas: Western meadowlark
Kentucky: Northern cardinal
Louisiana: Brown pelican
Maine: Chickadee
Maryland: Baltimore oriole
Massachusetts: Black-capped chickadee
Michigan: American robin
Minnesota: Common loon
Mississippi: Northern mockingbird
Missouri: Eastern bluebird
Montana: Western meadowlark
Nebraska: Western meadowlark
Nevada: Mountain bluebird
New Hampshire: Purple finch
New Jersey: Eastern goldfinch

New Mexico: Greater roadrunner
New York: Eastern bluebird
North Carolina: Northern cardinal
North Dakota: Western meadowlark
Ohio: Northern cardinal
Oklahoma: Scissor-tailed flycatcher
Oregon: Western meadowlark
Pennsylvania: Ruffed grouse
Rhode Island: Rhode Island Red
South Carolina: Carolina wren
South Dakota: Ring-necked pheasant
Tennessee: Northern mockingbird
Texas: Northern mockingbird
Utah: California gull
Vermont: Hermit thrush
Virginia: Northern cardinal
Washington: Willow goldfinch
West Virginia: Northern cardinal
Wisconsin: American robin
Wyoming: Western meadowlark

U.S. DISTRICT & TERRITORIES
Washington D.C.: Wood thrush
American Samoa: None
Guam: Guam rail
Northern Mariana Islands: Mariana fruit dove
Puerto Rico: Puerto Rican spindalis
U.S. Virgin Islands: Bananaquit

STATE TREES

Alabama: Longleaf pine
Alaska: Sitka spruce
Arizona: Blue palo verde
Arkansas: Loblolly pine
California: Coast redwood, giant Sequoia
Colorado: Colorado blue spruce
Connecticut: White oak
Delaware: American holly
Florida: Sabal palm
Georgia: Live oak
Hawaii: Candlenut tree
Idaho: Western white pine
Illinois: White oak
Indiana: Tulip tree
Iowa: Oak
Kansas: Eastern cottonwood
Kentucky: Tulip tree
Louisiana: Bald cypress
Maine: Eastern white pine
Maryland: White oak
Massachusetts: American elm
Michigan: Eastern white pine
Minnesota: Red pine
Mississippi: Southern magnolia
Missouri: Flowering dogwood
Montana: Ponderosa pine
Nebraska: Eastern cottonwood
Nevada: Single-leaf pinyon
New Hampshire: White birch
New Jersey: Northern red oak

New Mexico: Piñon pine
New York: Sugar maple
North Carolina: Pine
North Dakota: American elm
Ohio: Buckeye
Oklahoma: Eastern redbud
Oregon: Douglas fir
Pennsylvania: Eastern hemlock
Rhode Island: Red maple
South Carolina: Sabal palmetto
South Dakota: Black hills spruce
Tennessee: Tulip tree
Texas: Pecan
Utah: Quaking aspen
Vermont: Sugar maple
Virginia: Flowering dogwood
Washington: Western hemlock
West Virginia: Sugar maple
Wisconsin: Sugar maple
Wyoming: Plains cottonwood

U.S. DISTRICT & TERRITORIES
Washington D.C.: Scarlet oak
American Samoa: None
Guam: Pacific teak
Northern Mariana Islands: Flame tree
Puerto Rico: Kapok
U.S. Virgin Islands: Yellow trumpetbush

STATE FLOWERS

Alabama: Camellia
Alaska: Forget-me-not
Arizona: Saguaro cactus blossom
Arkansas: Apple blossom
California: California Poppy
Colorado: Colorado blue columbine
Connecticut: Mountain laurel
Delaware: Peach blossom
Florida: Orange blossom
Georgia: Cherokee rose
Hawaii: Hawaiian hibiscus
Idaho: Syringa
Illinois: Violet
Indiana: Peony
Iowa: Wild rose
Kansas: Sunflower
Kentucky: Goldenrod
Louisiana: Magnolia
Maine: White pine cone and tassel
Maryland: Black-eyed Susan
Massachusetts: Mayflower
Michigan: Apple blossom
Minnesota: Pink and white lady's slipper
Mississippi: Magnolia
Missouri: Hawthorn
Montana: Bitterroot
Nebraska: Goldenrod
Nevada: Sagebrush
New Hampshire: Purple lilac
New Jersey: Violet

New Mexico: Yucca flower
New York: Rose
North Carolina: Flowering dogwood
North Dakota: Wild prairie rose
Ohio: Scarlet carnation
Oklahoma: Oklahoma rose
Oregon: Oregon grape
Pennsylvania: Mountain laurel
Rhode Island: Violet
South Carolina: Yellow jessamine
South Dakota: Pasque flower
Tennessee: Iris
Texas: Bluebonnet
Utah: Sego lily
Vermont: Red clover
Virginia: Flowering dogwood
Washington: Coast rhododendron
West Virginia: Rhododendron
Wisconsin: Wood violet
Wyoming: Indian paintbrush

U.S. DISTRICT & TERRITORIES

Washington DC: American Beauty rose
American Samoa: Hala tree
Guam: Great bougainvillea
Northern Mariana Islands: Plumeria
Puerto Rico: Puerto Rican hibiscus
U.S. Virgin Islands: Yellow trumpetbush

(Some states also designate separate state wildflowers, which are not listed here.)

STATE GEMSTONES, ROCKS & MINERALS

Alabama: Star blue quartz (gemstone)
Alaska: Gold (mineral)
Arizona: Turquoise (gemstone)
Arkansas: Diamond (gemstone)
California: Gold (mineral)
Colorado: Aquamarine (gemstone)
Connecticut: Garnet (mineral)
Delaware: Sillimanite (mineral)
Florida: Moonstone (gemstone)
Georgia: Quartz (gemstone)
Hawaii: Black coral (gemstone)
Idaho: Star garnet (gemstone)
Illinois: Fluorite (mineral)
Indiana: Limestone (rock)
Iowa: Geode (rock)
Kansas: Galena (mineral)
Kentucky: Fresh water pearl (gemstone)
Louisiana: Agate (mineral)
Maine: Tourmaline (gemstone)
Maryland: Patuxent River stone agate (gemstone)
Massachusetts: Rhodonite (gemstone)
Michigan: Petoskey stone (rock)
Minnesota: Lake Superior agate (gemstone)
Mississippi: Petrified wood (rock)
Missouri: Galena (mineral)
Montana: Sapphire (gemstone)
Nebraska: Blue chalcedony (gemstone)
Nevada: Silver (metal)
New Hampshire: Smoky quartz (gemstone)

New Jersey: Franklinite (mineral)
New Mexico: Turquoise (gemstone)
New York: Garnet (gemstone)
North Carolina: Emerald (gemstone)
North Dakota: None
Ohio: Flint (gemstone)
Oklahoma: Barite rose (rock)
Oregon: Sunstone (gemstone)
Pennsylvania: None
Rhode Island: Bowenite (mineral)
South Carolina: Amethyst (gemstone)
South Dakota: Rose quartz (mineral)
Tennessee: Tennessee River pearl (gemstone)
Texas: Blue topaz (gemstone)
Utah: Topaz (gemstone)
Vermont: Grossular garnet (gemstone)
Virginia: Nelsonite (rock)
Washington: Petrified wood (gemstone)
West Virginia: Fossil coral (gemstone)
Wisconsin: Red granite (rock)
Wyoming: Jade (gemstone)

U.S. DISTRICT & TERRITORIES
Washington D.C.: Potomac bluestone (rock)
American Samoa: None
Guam: None
Northern Mariana Islands: None
Puerto Rico: None
U.S. Virgin Islands: None

(Some states designate separate state minerals, rocks, and gemstones, which are not all listed here.)

STATE FOSSILS

Alabama: Basilosaurus cetoides
Alaska: Woolly mammoth
Arizona: Petrified wood
California: Sabre-toothed cat
Colorado: Stegosaurus
Connecticut: Dinosaur tracks
Delaware: Belemnite
Florida: Agatized Coral
Georgia: Megalodon shark tooth
Idaho: Hagerman horse
Illinois: Tully monster
Indiana: American mastodon
Kansas: Pteranodon
Kentucky: Brachiopod
Louisiana: Petrified palm wood
Maine: Pertica quadrifaria
Maryland: Ecphora gardnerae
Massachusetts: Dinosaur tracks
Michigan: American mastodon
Mississippi: Prehistoric whale
Missouri: Sea lily
Nebraska: Mammoth
Nevada: Ichthyosaur
New Jersey: Hadrosaurus foulkii
New Mexico: Coelophysis
New York: Eurypterid
North Carolina: Megalodon shark tooth

North Dakota: Teredo petrified wood
Ohio: Trilobite
Oklahoma: Saurophaganax
Oregon: Dawn redwood
Pennsylvania: Trilobite
South Carolina: Columbian mammoth
South Dakota: Triceratops
Tennessee: Pterotrigonia
Texas: Paluxysaurus jonesi
Utah: Allosaurus
Vermont: Mount Holly mammoth
Virginia: Scallop
Washington: Columbian mammoth
West Virginia: Jefferson's ground sloth
Wisconsin: Trilobite
Wyoming: Knightia

U.S. DISTRICT & TERRITORIES

Washington D.C.: Capitalsaurus (dinosaur)
American Samoa: None
Guam: None
Northern Mariana Islands: None
Puerto Rico: None
U.S. Virgin Islands: None

EXCLUSIVE FREEBIE!

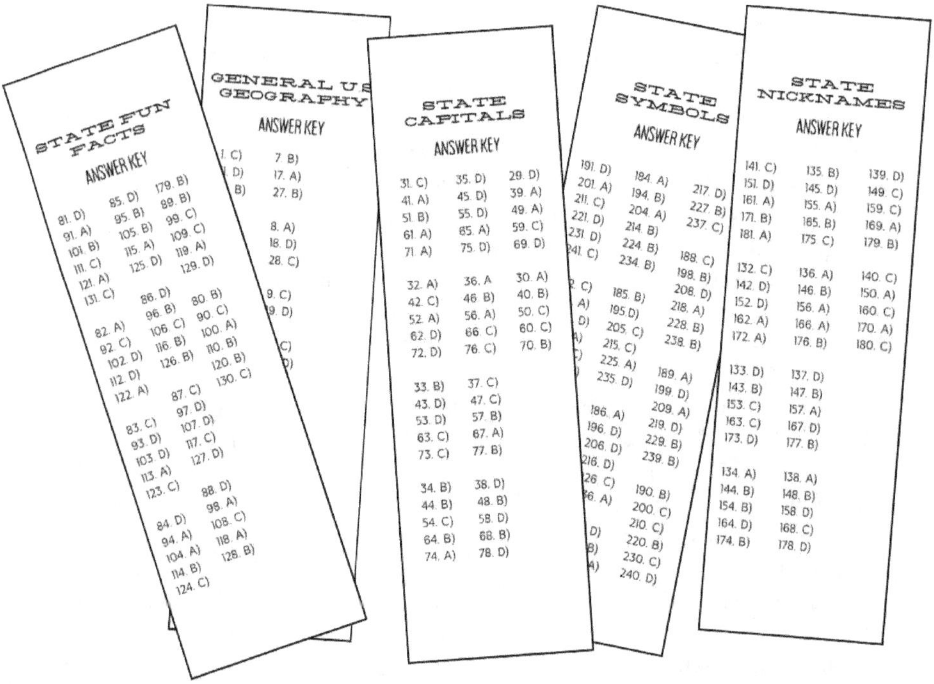

GET ALL THE ANSWERS AT YOUR FINGERTIPS!

DOWNLOAD FREE PRINTABLE ANSWER KEY BOOKMARKS

WHEN YOU SIGN UP FOR EMAILS!

Visit elizabethjameswrites.com/USAfreebie

ANSWERS

Please note that the answers on the following pages are intentionally arranged in a non-sequential pattern. For instance, the answers to questions 1, 11, 21, 31 and so forth are grouped together, followed by a group for questions 2, 12, 22, 32 and so on.

This deliberate arrangement is designed to prevent inadvertently seeing the answer to the next question when checking a response. We hope this ensures an exciting and engaging trivia experience while playing.

Enjoy the challenge!

GENERAL U.S. GEOGRAPHY

01. C)	23. A)	06. A)	28. C)
11. D)		16. A)	
21. B)	04. B)	26. D)	09. C)
	14. A)		19. D)
2. B)	24. C)	07. B)	
12. B)		17. A)	10. C)
22. B)	05. D)	27. B)	20. D)
	15. C)		
03. A)	25. B)	08. A)	
13. C)		18. D)	

STATE CAPITALS

31. C)	63. C)	36. A	68. B)
41. A)	73. C)	46. B)	78. D)
51. B)		56. A)	
61. A)	34. B)	66. C)	29. D)
71. A)	44. B)	76. C)	39. A)
	54. C)		49. A)
32. A)	64. B)	37. C)	59. C)
42. C)	74. A)	47. C)	69. D)
52. A)		57. B)	
62. D)	35. D)	67. A)	30. A)
72. D)	45. D)	77. B)	40. B)
	55. D)		50. C)
33. B)	65. A)	38. D)	60. C)
43. D)	75. D)	48. B)	70. B)
53. D)		58. D)	

FUN STATE FACTS

81. D)	103. D)	86. D)	118. A)
91. A)	113. A)	96. B)	128. B)
101. B)	123. C)	106. C)	79. B)
111. C)		116. B)	89. B)
121. A)	84. D)	126. B)	99. C)
131. C)	94. A)		109. C)
	104. A)	87. C)	119. A)
82. A)	114. B)	97. D)	129. D)
92. C)	124. C)	107. D)	
102. D)		117. C)	80. B)
112. D)	85. D)	127. D)	90. C)
122. A)	95. B)	88. D)	100. A)
	105. B)	98. A)	110. B)
83. C)	115. A)	108. C)	120. B)
93. D)	125. D)		130. C)

(ANSWERS CONTINUED ON NEXT PAGE)

STATE NICKNAMES

141. C)	173. D)	156. A)	
151. D)		166. A)	139. D)
161. A)	134. A)	176. B)	149. C)
171. B)	144. B)		159. C)
181. A)	154. B)	137. D)	169. A)
	164. D)	147. B)	179. B)
132. C)	174. B)	157. A)	
142. D)	135. B)	167. D)	140. C)
152. D)	145. D)	177. B)	150. A)
162. A)	155. A)		160. C)
172. A)	165. B)	138. A)	170. A)
133. D)	175. C)	148. B)	180. C)
143. B)		158. D)	
153. C)	136. A)	168. C)	
163. C)	146. B)	178. D)	

STATE SYMBOLS

191. D)	213. B)	186. A)	228. B)
201. A)	223. A)	196. D)	238. B)
211. C)	233. C)	206. D)	
221. D)	243. A)	216. D)	189. A)
231. D)		226. C)	199. D)
241. C)	184. A)	236. A)	209. A)
	194. B)		219. D)
182. C)	204. A)	187. D)	229. B)
192. A)	214. B)	197. B)	239. B)
202. D)	224. B)	207. A)	
212. A)	234. B)	217. D)	190. B)
222. C)		227. B)	200. C)
232. A)	185. B)	237. C)	210. C)
242. C)	195. D)		220. B)
	205. C)	188. C)	230. C)
183. D)	215. C)	198. B)	240. D)
193. C)	225. A)	208. D)	
203. B)	235. D)	218. A)	

www.ingramcontent.com/pod-product-compliance
Lightning Source LLC
Chambersburg PA
CBHW070728130626
46553CB00005B/2197